www.osha.gov

Occupational Safety and Health Act of 1970

"To assure safe and healthful working conditions for working men and women; by authorizing enforcement of the standards developed under the Act; by assisting and encouraging the States in their efforts to assure safe and healthful working conditions; by providing for research, information, education, and training in the field of occupational safety and health."

This publication provides a general overview of a particular standards-related topic. This publication does not alter or determine compliance responsibilities which are set forth in OSHA standards, and the *Occupational Safety and Health Act*. Moreover, because interpretations and enforcement policy may change over time, for additional guidance on OSHA compliance requirements, the reader should consult current administrative interpretations and decisions by the Occupational Safety and Health Review Commission and the courts.

This information will be made available to sensory impaired individuals upon request. Voice phone: (202) 693-1999; teletypewriter (TTY) number: 1-877-889-5627.

Guidance on
Preparing Workplaces
for an Influenza Pandemic

U.S. Department of Labor

Occupational Safety and Health Administration

OSHA 3327-05R
2009

Contents

Introduction

A pandemic is a global disease outbreak. An influenza pandemic occurs when a new influenza virus emerges for which there is little or no immunity in the human population, begins to cause serious illness and then spreads easily person-to-person worldwide. A worldwide influenza pandemic could have a major effect on the global economy, including travel, trade, tourism, food, consumption and eventually, investment and financial markets. Planning for pandemic influenza by business and industry is essential to minimize a pandemic's impact. Companies that provide critical infrastructure services, such as power and telecommunications, also have a special responsibility to plan for continued operation in a crisis and should plan accordingly. As with any catastrophe, having a contingency plan is essential.

In the event of an influenza pandemic, employers will play a key role in protecting employees' health and safety as well as in limiting the impact on the economy and society. Employers will likely experience employee absences, changes in patterns of commerce and interrupted supply and delivery schedules. Proper planning will allow employers in the public and private sectors to better protect their employees and lessen the impact of a pandemic on society and the economy. As stated in the President's *National Strategy for Pandemic Influenza*, all stakeholders must plan and be prepared.

The Occupational Safety and Health Administration (OSHA) developed this pandemic influenza planning guidance based upon traditional infection control and industrial hygiene practices. It is important to note that there is currently no pandemic; thus, this guidance is intended for planning purposes and is not specific to a particular viral strain. Additional guidance may be needed as an actual pandemic unfolds and more is known about the characteristics of the virulence of the virus, disease transmissibility, clinical manifestation, drug susceptibility, and risks to different age groups and subpopulations. Employers and employees should use this planning guidance to help identify risk levels in workplace settings and appropriate control measures that include good hygiene, cough etiquette, social distancing, the use of personal protective equipment, and staying home from work when ill. Up-to-date information and guidance is available to the public through the www.pandemicflu.gov website.

The Difference Between Seasonal, Pandemic Influenza and Avian Influenza

Seasonal influenza refers to the periodic outbreaks of respiratory illness in the fall and winter in the United States. Outbreaks are typically limited; most people have some immunity to the circulating strain of the virus. A vaccine is prepared in advance of the seasonal influenza; it is designed to match the influenza viruses most likely to be circulating in the community. Employees living abroad and international business travelers should note that other geographic areas (for example, the Southern Hemisphere) have different influenza seasons which may require different vaccines.

Pandemic influenza refers to a worldwide outbreak of influenza among people when a new strain of the virus emerges that has the ability to infect humans and to spread from person to person. During the early phases of an influenza pandemic, people might not have any natural immunity to the new strain; so the disease would spread rapidly among the population. A vaccine to protect people against illness from a pandemic influenza virus may not be widely available until many months after an influenza pandemic begins. It is important to emphasize that there currently is no influenza pandemic. However, pandemics have occurred throughout history and many scientists believe that it is only a matter of time before another one occurs. Pandemics can vary in severity from something that seems simply like a bad flu season to an especially severe influenza pandemic that could lead to high levels of illness, death, social disruption and economic loss. It is impossible to predict when the next pandemic will occur or whether it will be mild or severe.

Avian influenza (AI) – also known as the bird flu – is caused by virus that infects wild birds and domestic poultry. Some forms of the avian influenza are worse than others. Avian influenza viruses are generally divided into two groups: low pathogenic

5

avian influenza and highly pathogenic avian influenza. Low pathogenic avian influenza naturally occurs in wild birds and can spread to domestic birds. In most cases, it causes no signs of infection or only minor symptoms in birds. In general, these low path strains of the virus pose little threat to human health. Low pathogenic avian influenza virus H5 and H7 strains have the potential to mutate into highly pathogenic avian influenza and are, therefore, closely monitored. Highly pathogenic avian influenza spreads rapidly and has a high death rate in birds. Highly pathogenic avian influenza of the H5N1 strain is rapidly spreading in birds in some parts of the world.

Highly pathogenic H5N1 is one of the few avian influenza viruses to have crossed the species barrier to infect humans and it is the most deadly of those that have crossed the barrier. Most cases of H5N1 influenza infection in humans have resulted from contact with infected poultry or surfaces contaminated with secretions/excretions from infected birds.

As of February 2007, the spread of H5N1 virus from person to person has been limited to rare, sporadic cases. Nonetheless, because all influenza viruses have the ability to change, scientists are concerned that H5N1 virus one day could be able to sustain human to human transmission. Because these viruses do not commonly infect humans, there is little or no immune protection against them in the human population. If H5N1 virus were to gain the capacity to sustain transmission from person to person, a pandemic could begin.

An update on what is currently known about avian flu can be found at www.pandemicflu.gov.

How a Severe Pandemic Influenza Could Affect Workplaces

Unlike natural disasters or terrorist events, an influenza pandemic will be widespread, affecting multiple areas of the United States and other countries at the same time. A pandemic will also be an extended event, with multiple waves of outbreaks in the same geographic area; each outbreak could last from 6 to 8 weeks. Waves of outbreaks may occur over a year or more. Your workplace will likely experience:

- **Absenteeism** - A pandemic could affect as many as 40 percent of the workforce during periods of peak influenza illness. Employees could be absent because they are sick, must care for sick family members or for children if schools or day care centers are closed, are afraid to come to work, or the employer might not be notified that the employee has died.

- **Change in patterns of commerce** - During a pandemic, consumer demand for items related to infection control is likely to increase dramatically, while consumer interest in other goods may decline. Consumers may also change the ways in which they shop as a result of the pandemic. Consumers may try to shop at off-peak hours to reduce contact with other people, show increased interest in home delivery services, or prefer other options, such as drive-through service, to reduce person-to-person contact.

- **Interrupted supply/delivery** - Shipments of items from those geographic areas severely affected by the pandemic may be delayed or cancelled.

Who Should Plan for a Pandemic

To reduce the impact of a pandemic on your operations, employees, customers and the general public, it is important for all businesses and organizations to begin continuity planning for a pandemic now. Lack of continuity planning can result in a cascade of failures as employers attempt to address challenges of a pandemic with insufficient resources and employees who might not be adequately trained in the jobs they will be asked to perform. Proper planning will allow employers to better protect their employees and prepare for changing patterns of commerce and potential disruptions in supplies or services. Important tools for pandemic planning for employers are located at www.pandemicflu.gov.

The U.S. government has placed a special emphasis on supporting pandemic influenza planning for public and private sector businesses deemed to be critical industries and key resources (CI/KR). Critical infrastructure are the thirteen sectors that provide the production of essential goods and services, interconnectedness and operability, public safety, and security that contribute to a strong national defense and thriving economy. Key resources are facilities, sites, and groups of organized people whose destruction could cause large-scale injury, death, or destruction of property and/or profoundly damage our national prestige and confidence. With 85 percent of the nation's critical infrastructure in the hands of the private sector, the business community plays a vital role in ensuring national pandemic preparedness and response. Additional guidance for CI/KR business is available at: www.pandemicflu.gov/plan/pdf/CIKRpandemicInfluenzaGuide.pdf.

Critical Infrastructure and Key Resources

Key Resources

- Government Facilities
- Dams
- Commercial Facilities
- Nuclear Power Plants

Critical Infrastructure

- Food and Agriculture
- Public Health and Healthcare
- Banking and Finance
- Chemical and Hazardous Materials
- Defense Industrial Base
- Water
- Energy
- Emergency Services
- Information Technology
- Telecommunications
- Postal and Shipping
- Transportation
- National Monuments and Icons

How Influenza Can Spread Between People

Influenza is thought to be primarily spread through large droplets (droplet transmission) that directly contact the nose, mouth or eyes. These droplets are produced when infected people cough, sneeze or talk, sending the relatively large infectious droplets and very small sprays (aerosols) into the nearby air and into contact with other people. Large droplets can only travel a limited range; therefore, people should limit close contact (within 6 feet) with others when possible. To a lesser degree, human influenza is spread by touching objects contaminated with influenza viruses and then transferring the infected material from the hands to the nose, mouth or eyes. Influenza may also be spread by very small infectious particles (aerosols) traveling in the air. The contribution of each route of exposure to influenza transmission is uncertain at this time and may vary based upon the characteristics of the influenza strain.

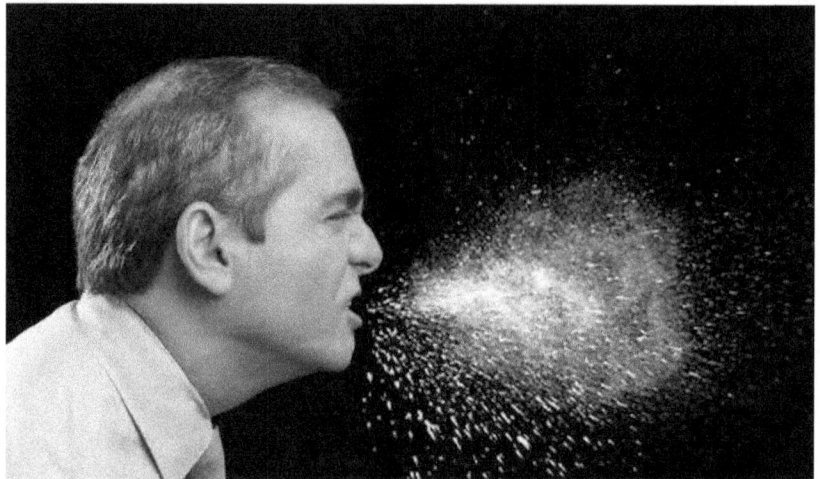

Fotosearch/Blend Images

Classifying Employee Exposure to Pandemic Influenza at Work

Employee risks of occupational exposure to influenza during a pandemic may vary from very high to high, medium, or lower (caution) risk. The level of risk depends in part on whether or not jobs require close proximity to people potentially infected with the pandemic influenza virus, or whether they are required to have either repeated or extended contact with known or suspected sources of pandemic influenza virus such as coworkers, the general public, outpatients, school children or other such individuals or groups.

- *Very high exposure risk* occupations are those with high potential exposure to high concentrations of known or suspected sources of pandemic influenza during specific medical or laboratory procedures.

- *High exposure risk* occupations are those with high potential for exposure to known or suspected sources of pandemic influenza virus.

- *Medium exposure risk* occupations include jobs that require frequent, close contact (within 6 feet) exposures to other people

(continued on page 12)

10

Occupational Risk Pyramid for Pandemic Influenza

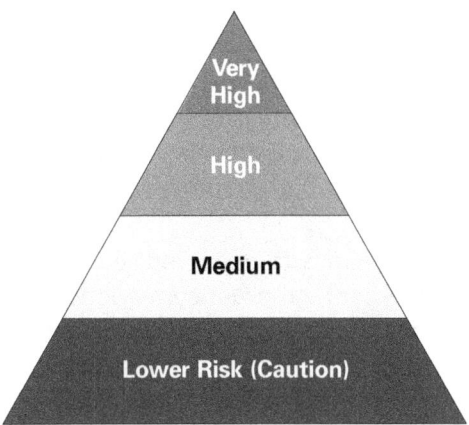

Very High Exposure Risk:
- Healthcare employees (for example, doctors, nurses, dentists) performing aerosol-generating procedures on known or suspected pandemic patients (for example, cough induction procedures, bronchoscopies, some dental procedures, or invasive specimen collection).
- Healthcare or laboratory personnel collecting or handling specimens from known or suspected pandemic patients (for example, manipulating cultures from known or suspected pandemic influenza patients).

High Exposure Risk:
- Healthcare delivery and support staff exposed to known or suspected pandemic patients (for example, doctors, nurses, and other hospital staff that must enter patients' rooms).
- Medical transport of known or suspected pandemic patients in enclosed vehicles (for example, emergency medical technicians).
- Performing autopsies on known or suspected pandemic patients (for example, morgue and mortuary employees).

Medium Exposure Risk:
- Employees with high-frequency contact with the general population (such as schools, high population density work environments, and some high volume retail).

Lower Exposure Risk (Caution):
- Employees who have minimal occupational contact with the general public and other coworkers (for example, office employees).

such as coworkers, the general public, outpatients, school children, or other such individuals or groups.

- *Lower exposure risk (caution)* occupations are those that do not require contact with people known to be infected with the pandemic virus, nor frequent close contact (within 6 feet) with the public. Even at lower risk levels, however, employers should be cautious and develop preparedness plans to minimize employee infections.

Employers of critical infrastructure and key resource employees (such as law enforcement, emergency response, or public utility employees) may consider upgrading protective measures for these employees beyond what would be suggested by their exposure risk due to the necessity of such services for the functioning of society as well as the potential difficulties in replacing them during a pandemic (for example, due to extensive training or licensing requirements).

To help employers determine appropriate work practices and precautions, OSHA has divided workplaces and work operations into four risk zones, according to the likelihood of employees' occupational exposure to pandemic influenza. We show these zones in the shape of a pyramid to represent how the risk will likely be distributed (see page 11). The vast majority of American workplaces are likely to be in the medium exposure risk or lower exposure risk (caution) groups.

How to Maintain Operations During a Pandemic

As an employer, you have an important role in protecting employee health and safety, and limiting the impact of an influenza pandemic. It is important to work with community planners to integrate your pandemic plan into local and state planning, particularly if your operations are part of the nation's critical infrastructure or key resources. Integration with local community planners will allow

you to access resources and information promptly to maintain operations and keep your employees safe.

Develop a Disaster Plan

Develop a disaster plan that includes pandemic preparedness (See www.pandemicflu.gov/plan/businesschecklist.html) and review it and conduct drills regularly.

- Be aware of and review federal, state and local health department pandemic influenza plans. Incorporate appropriate actions from these plans into workplace disaster plans.
- Prepare and plan for operations with a reduced workforce.
- Work with your suppliers to ensure that you can continue to operate and provide services.
- Develop a sick leave policy that does not penalize sick employees, thereby encouraging employees who have influenza-related symptoms (e.g., fever, headache, cough, sore throat, runny or stuffy nose, muscle aches, or upset stomach) to stay home so that they do not infect other employees. Recognize that employees with ill family members may need to stay home to care for them.
- Identify possible exposure and health risks to your employees. Are employees potentially in contact with people with influenza such as in a hospital or clinic? Are your employees expected to have a lot of contact with the general public?
- Minimize exposure to fellow employees or the public. For example, will more of your employees work from home? This may require enhancement of technology and communications equipment.
- Identify business-essential positions and people required to sustain business-necessary functions and operations. Prepare to cross-train or develop ways to function in the absence of these positions. It is recommended that employers train three or more employees to be able to sustain business-necessary functions and operations, and communicate the expectation for available employees to perform these functions if needed during a pandemic.

- Plan for downsizing services but also anticipate any scenario which may require a surge in your services.

- Recognize that, in the course of normal daily life, all employees will have non-occupational risk factors at home and in community settings that should be reduced to the extent possible. Some employees will also have individual risk factors that should be considered by employers as they plan how the organization will respond to a potential pandemic (e.g., immuno-compromised individuals and pregnant women).

- Stockpile items such as soap, tissue, hand sanitizer, cleaning supplies and recommended personal protective equipment. When stockpiling items, be aware of each product's shelf life and storage conditions (e.g., avoid areas that are damp or have temperature extremes) and incorporate product rotation (e.g., consume oldest supplies first) into your stockpile management program.

Make sure that your disaster plan protects and supports your employees, customers and the general public. Be aware of your employees' concerns about pay, leave, safety and health. Informed employees who feel safe at work are less likely to be absent.

- Develop policies and practices that distance employees from each other, customers and the general public. Consider practices to minimize face-to-face contact between employees such as e-mail, websites and teleconferences. Policies and practices that allow employees to work from home or to stagger their work shifts may be important as absenteeism rises.

- Organize and identify a central team of people or focal point to serve as a communication source so that your employees and customers can have accurate information during the crisis.

- Work with your employees and their union(s) to address leave, pay, transportation, travel, childcare, absence and other human resource issues.

- Provide your employees and customers in your workplace with easy access to infection control supplies, such as soap, hand sanitizers, personal protective equipment (such as gloves or surgical masks), tissues, and office cleaning supplies.

- Provide training, education and informational material about business-essential job functions and employee health and safety, including proper hygiene practices and the use of any personal protective equipment to be used in the workplace. Be sure that informational material is available in a usable format for individuals with sensory disabilities and/or limited English proficiency. Encourage employees to take care of their health by eating right, getting plenty of rest and getting a seasonal flu vaccination.

- Work with your insurance companies, and state and local health agencies to provide information to employees and customers about medical care in the event of a pandemic.

- Assist employees in managing additional stressors related to the pandemic. These are likely to include distress related to personal or family illness, life disruption, grief related to loss of family, friends or coworkers, loss of routine support systems, and similar challenges. Assuring timely and accurate communication will also be important throughout the duration of the pandemic in decreasing fear or worry. Employers should provide opportunities for support, counseling, and mental health assessment and referral should these be necessary. If present, Employee Assistance Programs can offer training and provide resources and other guidance on mental health and resiliency before and during a pandemic.

Protect Employees and Customers

Educate and train employees in proper hand hygiene, cough etiquette and social distancing techniques. Understand and develop work practice and engineering controls that could provide additional protection to your employees and customers, such as: drive-through service windows, clear plastic sneeze barriers, ventilation, and the proper selection, use and disposal of personal protective equipment.

These are not comprehensive recommendations. The most important part of pandemic planning is to work with your employees, local and state agencies and other employers to develop cooperative pandemic plans to maintain your operations

and keep your employees and the public safe. Share what you know, be open to ideas from your employees, then identify and share effective health practices with other employers in your community and with your local chamber of commerce.

How Organizations Can Protect Their Employees

For most employers, protecting their employees will depend on emphasizing proper hygiene (disinfecting hands and surfaces) and practicing social distancing (see page 26 for more information). Social distancing means reducing the frequency, proximity, and duration of contact between people (both employees and customers) to reduce the chances of spreading pandemic influenza from person-to-person. All employers should implement good hygiene and infection control practices.

Occupational safety and health professionals use a framework called the "hierarchy of controls" to select ways of dealing with workplace hazards. The hierarchy of controls prioritizes intervention strategies based on the premise that the best way to control a hazard is to systematically remove it from the workplace, rather than relying on employees to reduce their exposure. In the setting of a pandemic, this hierarchy should be used in concert with current public health recommendations. The types of measures that may be used to protect yourself, your employees, and your customers (listed from most effective to least effective) are: engineering controls, administrative controls, work practices, and personal protective equipment (PPE). Most employers will use a combination of control methods. There are advantages and disadvantages to each type of control measure when considering the ease of implementation, effectiveness, and cost. For example, hygiene and social distancing can be implemented relatively easily and with little expense, but this control method requires employees to modify and maintain their behavior, which may be difficult to sustain. On the other hand, installing clear plastic barriers or a drive-through window will be more expensive and take a longer

time to implement, although in the long run may be more effective at preventing transmission during a pandemic. Employers must evaluate their particular workplace to develop a plan for protecting their employees that may combine both immediate actions as well as longer term solutions.

Here is a description of each type of control:

Work Practice and Engineering Controls - Historically, infection control professionals have relied on personal protective equipment (for example, surgical masks and gloves) to serve as a physical barrier in order to prevent the transmission of an infectious disease from one person to another. This reflects the fact that close inter-actions with infectious patients is an unavoidable part of many healthcare occupations. The principles of industrial hygiene demonstrate that work practice controls and engineering controls can also serve as barriers to transmission and are less reliant on employee behavior to provide protection. Work practice controls are procedures for safe and proper work that are used to reduce the duration, frequency or intensity of exposure to a hazard. When defining safe work practice controls, it is a good idea to ask your employees for their suggestions, since they have firsthand experience with the tasks. These controls should be understood and followed by managers, supervisors and employees. When work practice controls are insufficient to protect employees, some employers may also need engineering controls.

Engineering controls involve making changes to the work environment to reduce work-related hazards. These types of controls are preferred over all others because they make permanent changes that reduce exposure to hazards and do not rely on employee or customer behavior. By reducing a hazard in the workplace, engineering controls can be the most cost-effective solutions for employers to implement.

During a pandemic, engineering controls may be effective in reducing exposure to some sources of pandemic influenza and not others. For example, installing sneeze guards between customers and employees would provide a barrier to transmission. The use of barrier protections, such as sneeze guards, is common practice for both infection control and industrial hygiene. However, while the

installation of sneeze guards may reduce or prevent transmission between customers and employees, transmission may still occur between coworkers. Therefore, administrative controls and public health measures should be implemented along with engineering controls.

Examples of work practice controls include:

- Providing resources and a work environment that promotes personal hygiene. For example, provide tissues, no-touch trash cans, hand soap, hand sanitizer, disinfectants and disposable towels for employees to clean their work surfaces.

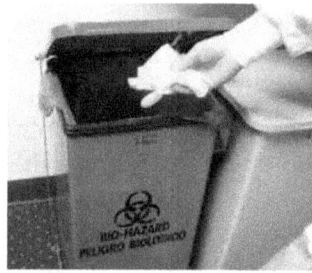

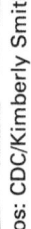

Additional photos: CDC/Kimberly Smith

- Encouraging employees to obtain a seasonal influenza vaccine (this helps to prevent illness from seasonal influenza strains that may continue to circulate).

- Providing employees with up-to-date education and training on influenza risk factors, protective behaviors, and instruction on proper behaviors (for example, cough ettiquette and care of personal protective equipment).

CDC/Jim Gathany

- Developing policies to minimize contacts between employees and between employees and clients or customers.

More information about protecting yourself, your coworkers and employees, and your family can be found at www.pandemicflu.gov.

Examples of engineering controls include:

- Installing physical barriers, such as clear plastic sneeze guards.

- Installing a drive-through window for customer service.

- In some limited healthcare settings, for aerosol generating procedures, specialized negative pressure ventilation may be indicated.

Administrative Controls - Administrative controls include controlling employees' exposure by scheduling their work tasks in ways that minimize their exposure levels. Examples of administrative controls include:

- Developing policies that encourage ill employees to stay at home without fear of any reprisals.

- The discontinuation of unessential travel to locations with high illness transmission rates.

- Consider practices to minimize face-to-face contact between employees such as e-mail, websites and teleconferences. Where possible, encourage flexible work arrangements such as telecommuting or flexible work hours to reduce the number of your employees who must be at work at one time or in one specific location.

- Consider home delivery of goods and services to reduce the number of clients or customers who must visit your workplace.

- Developing emergency communications plans. Maintain a forum for answering employees' concerns. Develop Internet-based communications if feasible.

Personal Protective Equipment (PPE) - While administrative and engineering controls and proper work practices are considered to be more effective in minimizing exposure to the influenza virus, the use of PPE may also be indicated during certain exposures. If used correctly, PPE can help prevent some exposures; however, they

should not take the place of other prevention interventions, such as engineering controls, cough etiquette, and hand hygiene (see www.cdc.gov/flu/protect/stopgerms.htm). Examples of personal protective equipment are gloves, goggles, face shields, surgical masks, and respirators (for example, N95). It is important that personal protective equipment be:

- Selected based upon the hazard to the employee;
- Properly fitted and some must be periodically refitted (e.g., respirators);
- Conscientiously and properly worn;
- Regularly maintained and replaced, as necessary;
- Properly removed and disposed of to avoid contamination of self, others or the environment.

Employers are obligated to provide their employees with protective gear needed to keep them safe while performing their jobs. The types of PPE recommended for pandemic influenza will be based on the risk of contracting influenza while working and the availability of PPE. Check the www.pandemicflu.gov website for the latest guidance.

The Difference Between a Facemask and a Respirator

It is important that employers and employees understand the significant differences between these types of personal protective equipment. The decision on whether or not to require employees to use either surgical/procedure masks or respirators must be based upon a hazard analysis of the employees' specific work environment and the differing protective properties of each type of personal protective equipment. The use of surgical masks or respirators is one component of infection control practices that may reduce transmission between infected and non-infected persons.

It should be noted that there is limited information on the use of surgical masks for the control of a pandemic in settings where there is no identified source of infection. There is no information on

respirator use in such scenarios since modern respirators did not exist during the last pandemic. However, respirators are now routinely used to protect employees against occupational hazards, including biological hazards such as tuberculosis, anthrax, and hantavirus. The effectiveness of surgical masks and respirators has been inferred on the basis of the mode of influenza transmission, particle size, and professional judgment.

To offer protection, both surgical masks and respirators must be worn correctly and consistently throughout the time they are being used. If used properly, surgical masks and respirators both have a role in preventing different types of exposures. During an influenza pandemic, surgical masks and respirators should be used in conjunction with interventions that are known to prevent the spread of infection, such as respiratory etiquette, hand hygiene, and avoidance of large gatherings.

Surgical Masks - Surgical masks are used as a physical barrier to protect employees from hazards such as splashes of large droplets of blood or body fluids. Surgical masks also prevent contamination by trapping large particles of body fluids that may contain bacteria or viruses when they are expelled by the wearer, thus protecting other people against infection from the person wearing the surgical mask.

Surgical/procedure masks are used for several different purposes, including the following:

- Placed on sick people to limit the spread of infectious respiratory secretions to others.

- Worn by healthcare providers to prevent accidental contamination of patients' wounds by the organisms normally present in mucus and saliva.

- Worn by employees to protect themselves from splashes or sprays of blood or body fluids; they may also have the effect of keeping contaminated fingers/hands away from the mouth and nose.

Surgical masks are not designed or certified to prevent the inhalation of small airborne contaminants. These small airborne contaminants are too little to see with the naked eye but may still be capable of causing infection. Surgical/procedure masks are not

designed to seal tightly against the user's face. During inhalation, much of the potentially contaminated air passes through gaps between the face and the surgical mask, thus avoiding being pulled through the material of the mask and losing any filtration that it may provide. Their ability to filter small particles varies significantly based upon the type of material used to make the surgical mask, and so they cannot be relied upon to protect employees against airborne infectious agents. Only surgical masks that are cleared by the U.S. Food and Drug Administration and legally marketed in the United States have been tested for their ability to resist blood and body fluids.

Respirators - Respirators are designed to reduce an employee's exposure to airborne contaminants. Respirators are designed to fit the face and to provide a tight seal between the respirator's edge and the face. A proper seal between the user's face and the respirator forces inhaled air to be pulled through the respirator's filter material and not through gaps between the face and respirator. Respirators must be used in the context of a comprehensive respiratory protection program, (see OSHA standard 29 CFR 1910.134, or www.osha.gov/SLTC/respiratoryprotection/index.html). It is important to medically evaluate employees to assure that they can perform work tasks while wearing a respirator. Medical evaluation can be as simple as a questionnaire (found in Appendix C of OSHA's Respiratory Protection standard, 29 CFR 1910.134). Employers who have never before needed to consider a respiratory protection plan should note that it can take time to choose a respirator to provide to employees and to arrange for a qualified trainer and provide training, fit testing, and medical evaluation for their employees. If employers wait until an influenza pandemic actually arrives, they may be unable to provide an adequate respiratory protection program in a timely manner.

Types of Respirators

Respirators can be air supplying (e.g., the self-contained breathing apparatus worn by firefighters) or air purifying (e.g., a gas mask that filters hazards from the air). Most employees affected by pandemic influenza who are deemed to need a respirator to minimize the likelihood of exposure to the pandemic influenza virus

in the workplace will use some type of air purifying respirator. They are also known as "particulate respirators" because they protect by filtering particles out of the air as you breathe. These respirators protect only against particles—not gases or vapors. Since airborne biological agents such as bacteria or viruses are particles, they can be filtered by particulate respirators.

Air purifying respirators can be divided into several types:

- *Filtering facepiece respirators*, where the entire respirator facepiece is comprised of filter material. This type of respirator is also commonly referred to as an "N95" respirator. It is discarded when it becomes unsuitable for further use due to excessive breathing resistance (e.g., particulate clogging the filter), unacceptable contamination/soiling, or physical damage.

  - *Surgical respirators* are a type of respiratory protection that offers the combined protective properties of both a filtering facepiece respirator and a surgical mask. Surgical N95 respirators are certified by NIOSH as respirators and also cleared by FDA as medical devices which have been designed and tested and shown to be equivalent to surgical masks in certain performance characteristics (resistance to blood penetration, biocompatibility) which are not examined by NIOSH during its certification of N95 respirators.

- *Reusable or elastomeric respirators*, where the facepiece can be cleaned, repaired and reused, but the filter cartridges are discarded and replaced when they become unsuitable for further use. These respirators come in half-mask (covering the mouth and nose) and full-mask (covering mouth, nose, and eyes) types. These respirators can be used with a variety of different cartridges to protect against different hazards. These respirators can also be used with canisters or cartridges that will filter out gases and vapors.

- *Powered air purifying respirators*, (PAPRs) where a battery-powered blower pulls contaminated air through filters, then moves the filtered air to the wearer's facepiece. PAPRs are significantly more expensive than other air purifying respirators but they provide higher levels of protection and may also increase the comfort for some users by reducing the physiologic burden

associated with negative pressure respirators and providing a constant flow of air on the face. These respirators can also be used with canisters or cartridges that will filter out gases and vapors. It should also be noted that there are hooded PAPRs that do not require employees to be fit tested in order to use them.

All respirators used in the workplace are required to be tested and certified by the National Institute for Occupational Safety and Health (NIOSH). NIOSH-certified respirators are marked with the manufacturer's name, the part number, the protection provided by the filter (e.g., N95), and "NIOSH." This information is printed on the facepiece, exhalation valve cover, or head straps. If a respirator does not have these markings it has not been certified by NIOSH. Those respirators that are surgical N95 respirators are also cleared by the FDA and, therefore, are appropriate for circumstances in which protection from airborne and body fluid contaminants is needed.

When choosing between disposable and reusable respirators, employers should consider their work environment, the nature of pandemics, and the potential for supply chain disruptions. Each pandemic influenza outbreak could last from 6 to 8 weeks and waves of outbreaks may occur over a year or more. While disposable respirators may be more convenient and cheaper on a per unit basis, a reusable respirator may be more economical on a long-term basis and reduce the impact of disruption in supply chains or shortages of respirators.

Classifying Particulate Respirators and Particulate Filters

An N95 respirator is one of nine types of particulate respirators. Respirator filters that remove at least 95 percent of airborne particles during "worst case" testing using the "most-penetrating" size of particle are given a 95 rating. Those that filter out at least 99 percent of the particles under the same conditions receive a 99 rating, and those that filter at least 99.97 percent (essentially 100 percent) receive a 100 rating.

In addition, filters in this family are given a designation of N, R, or P to convey their ability to function in the presence of oils that are found in some work environments.

"N" if they are <u>N</u>ot resistant to oil. (e.g., N95, N99, N100)

"R" if they are somewhat <u>R</u>esistant to oil. (e.g., R95, R99, R100)

"P" if they are strongly resistant (i.e., oil <u>P</u>roof). (e.g., P95, P99, P100)

This rating is important in work settings where oils may be present because some industrial oils can degrade the filter performance to the point that it does not filter adequately. Thus, the three filter efficiencies combined with the three oil designations lead to nine types of particulate respirator filter materials. It should be noted that any of the various types of filters listed here would be acceptable for protection against pandemic influenza in workplaces that do not contain oils, particularly if the N95 filter type was unavailable due to shortages.

Replacing Disposable Respirators

Disposable respirators are designed to be used once and are then to be properly disposed of. Once worn in the presence of an infectious patient, the respirator should be considered potentially contaminated with infectious material, and touching the outside of the device should be avoided to prevent self-inoculation (touching the contaminated respirator and then touching one's eyes, nose, or mouth). It should be noted that a once-worn respirator will also be contaminated on its inner surface by the microorganisms present in the exhaled air and oral secretions of the wearer.

If a sufficient supply of respirators is not available during a pandemic, employers and employees may consider reuse as long as the device has not been obviously soiled or damaged (e.g., creased or torn), and it retains its ability to function properly. This practice is not acceptable under normal circumstances and should only be considered under the most dire of conditions. Data on decontamination and/or reuse of respirators for infectious diseases are not available. Reuse may increase the potential for contamination; however, this risk must be balanced against the need to provide respiratory protection. When preparing for a pandemic, employers who anticipate providing respiratory protection to employees for the duration of the pandemic should consider using reusable or elastomeric respirators that are designed to be cleaned, repaired and reused.

Dust or Comfort Masks

Employers and employees should be aware that there are "dust" or "comfort" masks sold at home improvement stores that look very similar to respirators. Some dust masks may even be made by a manufacturer that also produces NIOSH-certified respirators. Unless a mask has been tested and certified by NIOSH, employers do not know if the device will filter very small airborne particles. The occupational use of respirators, including those purchased at home improvement or convenience stores, are still covered by OSHA's Respiratory Protection standard.

Note: Some respirators have an exhalation valve to make it easier for the wearer to breathe. While these respirators provide the same level of particle filtration protection to the wearer, they should not be used by healthcare providers who are concerned about contaminating a sterile field, or provided to known or suspected pandemic patients as a means of limiting the spread of their body fluids to others.

Note: Additional respirator and surgical mask guidance for healthcare workers has been developed and is available at www.pandemicflu.gov/plan/healthcare/maskguidancehc.html. This document, "Interim Guidance on Planning for the Use of Surgical Masks and Respirators in Health Care Settings during an Influenza Pandemic," provides details on the differences between a surgical mask and a respirator, the state of science regarding influenza transmission, and the rationale for determining the appropriate protective device.

Steps Every Employer Can Take to Reduce the Risk of Exposure to Pandemic Influenza in Their Workplace

The best strategy to reduce the risk of becoming infected with influenza during a pandemic is to avoid crowded settings and other situations that increase the risk of exposure to someone who may be infected. If it is absolutely necessary to be in a crowded setting,

the time spent in a crowd should be as short as possible. Some basic hygiene (see www.cdc.gov/flu/protect/stopgerms.htm) and social distancing precautions that can be implemented in every workplace include the following:

- Encourage sick employees to stay at home.

- Encourage your employees to wash their hands frequently with soap and water or with hand sanitizer if there is no soap or water available. Also, encourage your employees to avoid touching their noses, mouths, and eyes.

- Encourage your employees to cover their coughs and sneezes with a tissue, or to cough and sneeze into their upper sleeves if tissues are not available. All employees should wash their hands or use a hand sanitizer after they cough, sneeze or blow their noses.

- Employees should avoid close contact with their coworkers and customers (maintain a separation of at least 6 feet). They should avoid shaking hands and always wash their hands after contact with others. Even if employees wear gloves, they should wash their hands upon removal of the gloves in case their hand(s) became contaminated during the removal process.

- Provide customers and the public with tissues and trash receptacles, and with a place to wash or disinfect their hands.

- Keep work surfaces, telephones, computer equipment and other frequently touched surfaces and office equipment clean. Be sure that any cleaner used is safe and will not harm your employees or your office equipment. Use only disinfectants registered by the U.S. Environmental Protection Agency (EPA), and follow all directions and safety precautions indicated on the label.

- Discourage your employees from using other employees' phones, desks, offices or other work tools and equipment.

- Minimize situations where groups of people are crowded together, such as in a meeting. Use e-mail, phones and text messages to communicate with each other. When meetings are

necessary, avoid close contact by keeping a separation of at least 6 feet, where possible, and assure that there is proper ventilation in the meeting room.

- Reducing or eliminating unnecessary social interactions can be very effective in controlling the spread of infectious diseases. Reconsider all situations that permit or require employees, customers, and visitors (including family members) to enter the workplace. Workplaces which permit family visitors on site should consider restricting/eliminating that option during an influenza pandemic. Work sites with on-site day care should consider in advance whether these facilities will remain open or will be closed, and the impact of such decisions on employees and the business.

- Promote healthy lifestyles, including good nutrition, exercise, and smoking cessation. A person's overall health impacts their body's immune system and can affect their ability to fight off, or recover from, an infectious disease.

Workplaces Classified at Lower Exposure Risk (Caution) for Pandemic Influenza: What to Do to Protect Employees

If your workplace does not require employees to have frequent contact with the general public, basic personal hygiene practices and social distancing can help protect employees at work. Follow the general hygiene and social distancing practices previously recommended for all workplaces (see page 26). Also, try the following:

- Communicate to employees what options may be available to them for working from home.
- Communicate the office leave policies, policies for getting paid, transportation issues, and day care concerns.
- Make sure that your employees know where supplies for hand hygiene are located.

- Monitor public health communications about pandemic flu recommendations and ensure that your employees also have access to that information.
- Work with your employees to designate a person(s), website, bulletin board or other means of communicating important pandemic flu information.

   More information about protecting employees and their families can be found at: www.pandemicflu.gov.

Workplaces Classified at Medium Exposure Risk for Pandemic Influenza: What to Do to Protect Employees

Medium risk workplaces require frequent close contact between employees or with the general public (such as high-volume retail stores). If this contact cannot be avoided, there are practices to reduce the risk of infection. In addition to the basic work practices that every workplace should adopt (see page 26), medium risk occupations require employers to address enhanced safety and health precautions. Below are some of the issues that employers should address when developing plans for workplace safety and health during a pandemic.

Work Practice and Engineering Controls
- Instruct employees to avoid close contact (within 6 feet) with other employees and the general public. This can be accomplished by simply increasing the distance between the employee and the general public in order to avoid contact with large droplets from people talking, coughing or sneezing.
- Some organizations can expand internet, phone-based, drive-through window, or home delivery customer service strategies to minimize face-to-face contact. Work with your employees to identify new ways to do business that can also help to keep employees and customers safe and healthy.

- Communicate the availability of medical screening or other employee health resources (e.g., on-site nurse or employee wellness program to check for flu-like symptoms before employees enter the workplace).
- Employers also should consider installing physical barriers, such as clear plastic sneeze guards, to protect employees where possible (such as cashier stations).

Administrative Controls

- Work with your employees so that they understand the office leave policies, policies for getting paid, transportation issues, and day care concerns.
- Make sure that employees know where supplies for hand and surface hygiene are located.
- Work with your employees to designate a person(s), website, bulletin board or other means of communicating important pandemic flu information.
- Use signs to keep customers informed about symptoms of the flu, and ask sick customers to minimize contact with your employees until they are well.
- Your workplace may consider limiting access to customers and the general public, or ensuring that they can only enter certain areas of your workplace.

Personal Protective Equipment (PPE)

Employees who have high-frequency, close contact with the general population that cannot be eliminated using administrative or engineering controls, and where contact with symptomatic ill persons is not expected should use personal protective equipment to prevent sprays of potentially infected liquid droplets (from talking, coughing, or sneezing) from contacting their nose or mouth. A surgical mask will provide such barrier protection. Use of a respirator may be considered if there is an expectation of close contact with persons who have symptomatic influenza infection or if employers choose to provide protection against a risk of airborne transmission. It should be noted that wearing a respirator may be

physically burdensome to employees, particularly when the use of PPE is not common practice for the work task. In the event of a shortage of surgical masks, a reusable face shield that can be decontaminated may be an acceptable method of protecting against droplet transmission of an infectious disease but will not protect against airborne transmission, to the extent that disease may spread in that manner.

Eye protection generally is not recommended to prevent influenza infection although there are limited examples where strains of influenza have caused eye infection (conjunctivitis). At the time of a pandemic, health officials will assess whether risk of conjunctival infection or transmission exists for the specific pandemic viral strain.

Employees should wash hands frequently with soap or sanitizing solutions to prevent hands from transferring potentially infectious material from surfaces to their mouths or noses. While employers and employees may choose to wear gloves, the exposure of concern is touching the mouth and nose with a contaminated hand and not exposure to the virus through non-intact skin (for example, cuts or scrapes). While the use of gloves may make employees more aware of potential hand contamination, there is no difference between intentional or unintentional touching of the mouth, nose or eyes with either a contaminated glove or a contaminated hand. If an employee does wear gloves, they should always wash their hands with soap or sanitizing solution immediately after removal to ensure that they did not contaminate their hand(s) while removing them.

When selecting PPE, employers should consider factors such as function, fit, ability to be decontaminated, disposal, and cost. Sometimes, when a piece of PPE will have to be used repeatedly for a long period of time, a more expensive and durable piece of PPE may be less expensive in the long run than a disposable piece of PPE. For example, in the event of a pandemic, there may be shortages of surgical masks. A reusable face shield that can be decontaminated may become the preferred method of protecting against droplet transmission in some workplaces. It should be noted that barrier protection, such as a surgical mask or face shield, will protect against droplet transmission of an infectious disease

but will not protect against airborne transmission, to the extent that the disease may be spread in that manner. Each employer should select the combination of PPE that protects employees in their particular workplace. It should also be noted that wearing PPE may be physically burdensome to employees, particularly when the use of PPE is not common practice for the work task.

Educate and train employees about the protective clothing and equipment appropriate to their current duties and the duties which they may be asked to assume when others are absent. Employees may need to be fit tested and trained in the proper use and care of a respirator. Also, it is important to train employees to put on (don) and take off (doff) PPE in the proper order to avoid inadvertent self-contamination (www.osha.gov/SLTC/respiratoryprotection/index.html). During a pandemic, recommendations for PPE use in particular occupations may change, depending on geographic proximity to active cases, updated risk assessments for particular employees, and information on PPE effectiveness in preventing the spread of influenza.

Workplaces Classified at Very High or High Exposure Risk for Pandemic Influenza: What to Do to Protect Employees

If your workplace requires your employees to have contact with people that are known or suspected to be infected with the pandemic virus, there are many practices that can be used to reduce the risk of infection and to protect your employees. Additional guidance for very high and high exposure risk workplaces, such as healthcare facilities, can be found at: www.pandemicflu.gov and www.osha.gov.

Very high and high exposure risk occupations require employers to address enhanced safety and health precautions in addition to the basic work practices that every workplace should adopt (see page 26). Employers should also be aware that working in a high

risk occupation can be stressful to both employees and their families. Employees in high risk occupations may have heightened concern about their own safety and possible implications for their family. Such workplaces may experience greater employee absenteeism than other lower risk workplaces. Talk to your employees about resources that can help them in the event of a pandemic crisis. Keeping the workplace safe is everyone's priority. More information about protecting employees and their families can be found at: www.pandemicflu.gov.

Work Practice and Engineering Controls

Employers should ensure that employees have adequate training and supplies to practice proper hygiene. Emergency responders and other essential personnel who may be exposed while working away from fixed facilities should be provided with hand sanitizers that do not require water so that they can decontaminate themselves in the field. Employers should work with employees to identify ways to modify work practices to promote social distancing and prevent close contact (within 6 feet), where possible. Employers should also consider offering enhanced medical monitoring of employees in very high and high risk work environments.

In certain limited circumstances ventilation is recommended for high and very high risk work environments. While proper ventilation can reduce the risk of transmission for healthcare workers in the same room as infectious patients, it cannot be relied upon as the sole protective measure. Thus, a combination of engineering controls and personal protective equipment will be needed.

- When possible, healthcare facilities equipped with isolation rooms should use them when performing aerosol generating procedures for patients with known or suspected pandemic influenza.

- Laboratory facilities that handle specimens for known or suspected pandemic patients will also require special precautions associated with a Bio-Safety Level 3 facility. Some recommendations can be found at: www.cdc.gov/flu/h2n2bs13.htm.

Employers should also consider installing physical barriers, such as clear plastic sneeze guards, to protect employees where possible (for example, reception or intake areas). The use of barrier protections,

such as sneeze guards, is common practice for both infection control and industrial hygiene.

Administrative Controls (Isolation Precautions)

If working in a healthcare facility, follow existing guidelines and facility standards of practice for identifying and isolating infected individuals and for protecting employees. See the U.S. Department of Health and Human Services' pandemic influenza plan for health-care facilities at: www.hhs.gov/pandemicflu/plan/sup4.html.

Personal Protective Equipment (PPE)

Those who work closely with (either in contact with or within 6 feet) people known or suspected to be infected with pandemic influenza virus should wear:

- Respiratory protection for protection against small droplets from talking, coughing or sneezing and also from small airborne particles of infectious material.
  - N95 or higher rated filter for most situations.
  - Supplied air respirator (SAR) or powered air purifying respirator (PAPR) for certain high risk medical or dental procedures likely to generate bioaerosols.
  - Use a surgical respirator when both respiratory protection and resistance to blood and body fluids is necessary.
- Face shields may also be worn on top of a respirator to prevent bulk contamination of the respirator. Certain respirator designs with forward protrusions (duckbill style) may be difficult to properly wear under a face shield. Ensure that the face shield does not prevent airflow through the respirator.
- Medical/surgical gowns or other disposable/decontaminable protective clothing.
- Gloves to reduce transfer of infectious material from one patient to another.
- Eye protection if splashes are anticipated.

The appropriate form of respirator will depend on the type of exposure and on the transmission pattern of the particular strain of

influenza. See the National Institute for Occupational Safety and Health (NIOSH) Respirator Selection Logic at: www.cdc.gov/niosh/docs/2005-100.

Educate and train employees about the protective clothing and equipment appropriate to their current duties and the duties which they may be asked to assume when others are absent. Education and training material should be easy to understand and available in the appropriate language and literacy level for all employees. Employees need to be fit tested and trained in the proper use and care of a respirator. It is also important to train employees to put on (don) and take off (doff) PPE in the proper order to avoid inadvertent self-contamination (www.osha.gov/SLTC/respiratoryprotection/index.html). Employees who dispose of PPE and other infectious waste must also be trained and provided with appropriate PPE.

During a pandemic, recommendations for PPE use in particular occupations may change depending on geographic location, updated risk assessments for particular employees, and information on PPE effectiveness in preventing the spread of influenza. Additional respirator and surgical mask guidance for healthcare workers has been developed and is available at www.pandemicflu.gov/plan/healthcare/maskguidancehc.html. This document, *Interim Guidance on Planning for the Use of Surgical Masks and Respirators in Health Care Settings during an Influenza Pandemic*, provides details on the differences between a surgical mask and a respirator, the state of science regarding influenza transmission, and the rationale for determining the appropriate protective device.

What Employees Living Abroad or Who Travel Internationally for Work Should Know

Employees living abroad and international business travelers should note that other geographic areas have different influenza seasons and will likely be affected by a pandemic at different times than the United States. The U.S. Department of State emphasizes that, in the event of a pandemic, its ability to assist Americans traveling and

residing abroad may be severely limited by restrictions on local and international movement imposed for public health reasons, either by foreign governments and/or the United States. Furthermore, American citizens should take note that the Department of State cannot provide Americans traveling or living abroad with medications or supplies even in the event of a pandemic.

In addition, the Department of State has asked its embassies and consulates to consider preparedness measures that take into consideration the fact that travel into or out of a country may not be possible, safe, or medically advisable during a pandemic. Guidance on how private citizens can prepare to shelter in place, including stocking food, water, and medical supplies, is available at the www.pandemicflu.gov website. Embassy stocks cannot be made available to private American citizens abroad, therefore, employers and employees are encouraged to prepare appropriately. It is also likely that governments will respond to a pandemic by imposing public health measures that restrict domestic and international movement, further limiting the U.S. government's ability to assist Americans in these countries. As it is possible that these measures may be implemented very quickly, it is important that employers and employees plan appropriately.

More information on pandemic influenza planning for employees living and traveling abroad can be found at:

www.pandemicflu.gov/travel/index.html

www.cdc.gov/travel

www.state.gov/travelandbusiness

For More Information

Federal, state and local government agencies are your best source of information should an influenza pandemic take place. It is important to stay informed about the latest developments and recommendations since specific guidance may change based upon the characteristics of the eventual pandemic influenza strain, (for example, severity of disease, importance of various modes of transmission).

Below are several recommended websites that you can rely on for the most current and accurate information:

www.pandemicflu.gov
(Managed by the U.S. Department of Health and Human Services; offers one-stop access, including toll-free phone numbers, to U.S. government avian and pandemic flu information.)

www.osha.gov
(Occupational Safety and Health Administration website)

www.cdc.gov/niosh
(National Institute for Occupational Safety and Health website)

www.cdc.gov
(Centers for Disease Control and Prevention website)

www.fda.gov/cdrh/ppe/fluoutbreaks.html
(U.S. Food and Drug Administration website)

OSHA Assistance

OSHA can provide extensive help through a variety of programs, including technical assistance about effective safety and health programs, state plans, workplace consultations, and training and education.

Safety and Health Program Management Guidelines

Effective management of worker safety and health protection is a decisive factor in reducing the extent and severity of work-related injuries and illnesses and their related costs. In fact, an effective safety and health management system forms the basis of good worker protection, can save time and money, increase productivity and reduce employee injuries, illnesses and related workers' compensation costs.

To assist employers and workers in developing effective safety and health management system, OSHA published recommended *Safety and Health Program Management Guidelines* (54 *Federal Register* (16): 3904-3916, January 26, 1989). These voluntary guidelines can be applied to all places of employment covered by OSHA.

The guidelines identify four general elements critical to the development of a successful safety and health management system:

- Management leadership and worker involvement,
- Worksite analysis,
- Hazard prevention and control, and
- Safety and health training.

The guidelines recommend specific actions, under each of these general elements, to achieve an effective safety and health system. The *Federal Register* notice is available online at www.osha.gov.

State Programs

The Occupational Safety and Health Act of 1970 (OSH Act) encourages states to develop and operate their own job safety and health plans. OSHA approves and monitors these plans. Twenty-four states, Puerto Rico and the Virgin Islands currently

operate approved state plans: 22 cover both private and public (state and local government) employment; Connecticut, New Jersey, New York and the Virgin Islands cover the public sector only. States and territories with their own OSHA-approved occupational safety and health plans must adopt standards identical to, or at least as effective as, the Federal OSHA standards.

Consultation Services

Consultation assistance is available on request to employers who want help in establishing and maintaining a safe and healthful workplace. Largely funded by OSHA, the service is provided at no cost to the employer. Primarily developed for smaller employers with more hazardous operations, the consultation service is delivered by state governments employing professional safety and health consultants. Comprehensive assistance includes an appraisal of all mechanical systems, work practices, and occupational safety and health hazards of the workplace and all aspects of the employer's present job safety and health program. In addition, the service offers assistance to employers in developing and implementing an effective safety and health program. No penalties are proposed or citations issued for hazards identified by the consultant. OSHA provides consultation assistance to the employer with the assurance that his or her name and firm and any information about the workplace will not be routinely reported to OSHA enforcement staff. For more information concerning consultation assistance, see OSHA's website at www.osha.gov.

Strategic Partnership Program

OSHA's Strategic Partnership Program helps encourage, assist and recognize the efforts of partners to eliminate serious workplace hazards and achieve a high level of worker safety and health. Most strategic partnerships seek to have a broad impact by building cooperative relationships with groups of employers and workers. These partnerships are voluntary relationships between OSHA, employers, worker representatives, and others (e.g., trade unions, trade and professional associations, universities, and other government agencies).

For more information on this and other agency programs, contact your nearest OSHA office, or visit OSHA's website at www.osha.gov.

OSHA Training and Education

OSHA area offices offer a variety of information services, such as technical advice, publications, audiovisual aids and speakers for special engagements. OSHA's Training Institute in Arlington Heights, IL, provides basic and advanced courses in safety and health for Federal and state compliance officers, state consultants, Federal agency personnel, and private sector employers, workers and their representatives.

The OSHA Training Institute also has established OSHA Training Institute Education Centers to address the increased demand for its courses from the private sector and from other federal agencies. These centers are colleges, universities, and nonprofit organizations that have been selected after a competition for participation in the program.

OSHA also provides funds to nonprofit organizations, through grants, to conduct workplace training and education in subjects where OSHA believes there is a lack of workplace training. Grants are awarded annually.

For more information on grants, training and education, contact the OSHA Training Institute, Directorate of Training and Education, 2020 South Arlington Heights Road, Arlington Heights, IL 60005, (847) 297-4810, or see Training on OSHA's website at www.osha.gov. For further information on any OSHA program, contact your nearest OSHA regional office listed at the end of this publication.

Information Available Electronically

OSHA has a variety of materials and tools available on its website at www.osha.gov. These include electronic tools, such as Safety and Health Topics, eTools, Expert Advisors; regulations, directives and publications; videos and other information for employers and workers. OSHA's software programs and eTools walk you through challenging safety and health issues and common problems to find the best solutions for your workplace.

OSHA Publications

OSHA has an extensive publications program. For a listing of free items, visit OSHA's website at www.osha.gov or contact the OSHA Publications Office, U.S. Department of Labor, 200 Constitution

Avenue, NW, N-3101, Washington, DC 20210; telephone (202) 693-1888 or fax to (202) 693-2498.

Contacting OSHA

To report an emergency, file a complaint, or seek OSHA advice, assistance, or products, call (800) 321-OSHA or contact your nearest OSHA Regional or Area office listed at the end of this publication. The teletypewriter (TTY) number is (877) 889-5627.

Written correspondence can be mailed to the nearest OSHA Regional or Area Office listed at the end of this publication or to OSHA's national office at: U.S. Department of Labor, Occupational Safety and Health Administration, 200 Constitution Avenue, N.W., Washington, DC 20210.

By visiting OSHA's website at www.osha.gov, you can also:

- File a complaint online,
- Submit general inquiries about workplace safety and health electronically, and
- Find more information about OSHA and occupational safety and health.

(OOC 5/2009)

www.osha.gov

OSHA Regional Offices

Region I
(CT,* ME, MA, NH, RI, VT*)
JFK Federal Building, Room E340
Boston, MA 02203
(617) 565-9860

Region II
(NJ,* NY,* PR,* VI*)
201 Varick Street, Room 670
New York, NY 10014
(212) 337-2378

Region III
(DE, DC, MD,* PA, VA,* WV)
The Curtis Center
170 S. Independence Mall West
Suite 740 West
Philadelphia, PA 19106-3309
(215) 861-4900

Region IV
(AL, FL, GA, KY,* MS, NC,* SC,* TN*)
61 Forsyth Street, SW, Room 6T50
Atlanta, GA 30303
(404) 562-2300

Region V
(IL, IN,* MI,* MN,* OH, WI)
230 South Dearborn Street
Room 3244
Chicago, IL 60604
(312) 353-2220

Region VI
(AR, LA, NM,* OK, TX)
525 Griffin Street, Room 602
Dallas, TX 75202
(972) 850-4145

Region VII
(IA,* KS, MO, NE)
Two Pershing Square
2300 Main Street, Suite 1010
Kansas City, MO 64108-2416
(816) 283-8745

Region VIII
(CO, MT, NO, SO, UT,* WY*)
1999 Broadway, Suite 1690
PO Box 46550
Denver, CO 80202-5716
(720) 264-6550

Region IX
(AZ,* CA,* HI,* NV,* and American
Samoa,
Guam and the Northern Mariana
Islands)
90 7th Street, Suite 18-100
San Francisco, CA 94103
(415) 625-2547

Region X
(AK,* ID, OR,* WA*)
1111 Third Avenue, Suite 715
Seattle, WA 98101-3212
(206) 553-5930

* These states and territories operate their own OSHA-approved job safety and health programs and cover state and local government employees as well as private sector employees. The Connecticut, New Jersey, New York and Virgin Islands plans cover public employees only. States with approved programs must have standards that are identical to, or at least as effective as, the Federal OSHA standards.

Note: To get contact information for OSHA Area Offices, OSHA-approved State Plans and OSHA Consultation Projects, please visit us online at www.osha.gov or call us at 1-800-321-0SHA.

www.ingramcontent.com/pod-product-compliance
Lightning Source LLC
Chambersburg PA
CBHW051824170526
45167CB00005B/2142

* 9 7 8 1 4 9 7 3 8 8 5 0 5 *